Docklands
Light Railway
Official Handbook

Alan Pearce

Brian Hardy

Colin Stannard

Capital Transport

Fifth edition 2006

ISBN 185414 298 4

Published by Capital Transport Publishing
PO Box 250, Harrow, Middlesex

Printed by Thomson Press, Harrow, Middlesex

Photographic credits

Alan Blake 37

Capital Transport 1, 3, 14, 16, 17, 18, 19, 20, 21, 22, 23, 24,
25, 26, 27, 28, 30, 31, 32, 33, 34, 36, 38, 39, 40, 41, 43, 48,
49, 53, 58

DLR 15, 29, 35, 45, 46, 50, 57, 61

Frank Hornby 62

Alan Pearce 4, 6, 9, 10, 11

Contents

Canary Wharf in 1986, with construction of the DLR in progress.

Right A London Transport study of 1981 of light rail options for Docklands. A line to Beckton had appeared in a map produced the previous year and was to be revived in 1982. Street running is included to Mile End and a short tube tunnel loop terminus at Aldgate East or Tower Hill. Conversion of the East London Line to light rail was also listed as a possibility.

Origins of the DLR

The closure of London's up-river docks had left the capital with an area of about 8½ square miles with all the signs of urban dereliction; the jobs had gone or moved downstream to container handling ports like Tilbury, public transport had declined and social, retail and leisure facilities had either gone or had not kept pace with the type, quantity and quality appearing elsewhere in London.

In 1972, the London Docklands Study Team commissioned Travers Morgan & Partners to investigate and report on ideas for the redevelopment of the area. Whilst the report, published in January 1973, saw a future demand for better public transport to serve the Isle of Dogs peninsula, this was thought to be insufficient to justify a new conventional railway, let alone an Underground line. Instead, a low cost 'minitram' peoplemover system with vehicles carrying up to 20 people each was seen as the answer to connect Docklands with the proposed Fleet Line at Fenchurch Street.

In 1974 the Docklands Joint Committee was formed by the Greater London Council, along with the Boroughs of Greenwich, Lewisham, Newham, Southwark and Tower Hamlets. Its object was to develop Docklands as quickly as

possible, with a combination of new industry and housing. The committee reviewed the existing state of local public transport and examined the possibilities for improvement to suit the needs of the new development. Two light rail options were considered, one terminating at Tower Hill (District and Circle Lines interchange) and the other at Fenchurch Street (then a proposed Fleet Line interchange), but both of these options were considered too expensive.

A 1976 report recommended early construction of an Underground line to serve the area and parliamentary powers were obtained by London Transport for a tube connection from Charing Cross via Fenchurch Street, Surrey Docks, Isle of Dogs, North Greenwich and Custom House to Woolwich Arsenal.

However, things changed rapidly and radically when Margaret Thatcher's Conservative government took office on 4th May 1979. As early as June of that year, Norman Fowler as the new Minister of Transport put the brakes on commitment to the construction of a tube through or near Docklands for reasons of financial restraint. The government insisted that a review of lower cost options for Docklands be undertaken.

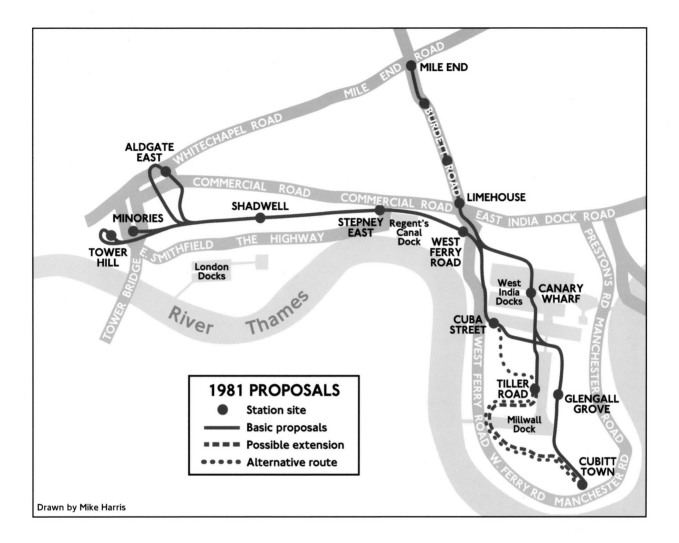

1981 PROPOSALS
- ● Station site
- —— Basic proposals
- ▬ ▬ ▬ Possible extension
- • • • • • Alternative route

Drawn by Mike Harris

Most of the options looked at were not new, but a most significant development was a recommendation to check out the feasibility of a fully segregated automatic light rail system from Aldgate East to the Isle of Dogs and on to Beckton.

A plan drawn up as a result of this envisaged 13 stations on a 13 km double-track line, 1 km of which was to be in tube at the Aldgate end, and a depot at Beckton. It was the formation of the London Docklands Development Corporation (LDDC) in July 1981 that was to inject new urgency into the need for a decision. Soon after the LDDC was formed, it commissioned London Transport to study ways of introducing a low-cost rail-based solution to satisfy the needs of the development.

A desirable answer would have been to link a light rail metro into either the District/Metropolitan at Aldgate East or somewhere further east, or the District/Circle at Tower Hill, to connect Docklands directly with a multiplicity of central area destinations. It soon became clear that capacity problems on the existing train paths would not permit light rail trains joining the system at any of those points. There was the possibility of using the East London Line in the Docklands solution, but this also was effectively divorced from the rest of the Underground for the same reasons. Because direct integration of the new line into the main system looked impossible, there was therefore no reason to make the new facility compatible with the existing Underground network.

5

One of the simplest options viewed for the east/west line was to install street tramway from Aldgate East all along the Commercial Road to Limehouse. A variant was to use a central alignment along The Highway on the level, which could have been at least segregated from the street, although how this would lock into the scheme east of Limehouse was uncertain.

Three possible city termini were viewed, although a low level interchange beside the existing Underground station at Tower Hill was ruled out at an early stage because it would have been very costly to construct in such a way as to avoid undue congestion. The two more feasible alternatives were a low level interchange station at Aldgate East or a high level terminus at Minories. It was the latter that eventually became the Tower Gateway terminus of the DLR.

It made sense to adapt the existing BR viaduct from Fenchurch Street to what was then called Stepney East Station (today Limehouse). BR had indicated that their utilisation of the viaduct could be pruned to two tracks apart from the immediate approach to Fenchurch Street Station. Therefore a new section of viaduct would be needed from Cannon Street Road into the new elevated Minories terminus. If the Tower Hill option had been feasible, a 5% ramp to tunnels would have started from Cannon Street Road

leading to a loop about 10 metres below the District/Circle platforms. Escalators would have led up to these platforms and the existing exit would have been shared between Underground and light rail passengers. Likewise, if Aldgate East had been the terminus, the ramp to tunnels would have started at Cannon Street Road, leading to a loop with a single platform at some 90 degrees to and 13 metres beneath the District/Hammersmith & City platforms. Exit to the street would have been via the Underground platform and either existing ticket hall.

Eastward from Stepney East, the disused London & Blackwall railway viaduct beckoned. On the Isle of Dogs two possibilities existed – a 'western' route running across Millwall Docks Cut to Cubitt Town, or a 'central' route right down the middle of the peninsula, dependent on the West India Docks being infilled or bridged. The 'western' route would have left the London & Blackwall viaduct immediately east of West Ferry Road to more or less parallel that road southwards before turning eastwards to pick up the line of the old dock railway to serve a station at Cuba Street. From there, Millwall Dock cut could have been crossed by a lifting bridge, with a light rail station placed at East Ferry Road/Glengall Grove. A terminus was planned for Manchester Road, Cubitt Town, reached by reuse of the derelict viaduct following refurbishment.

A view south of All Saints DLR station during the railway's construction.

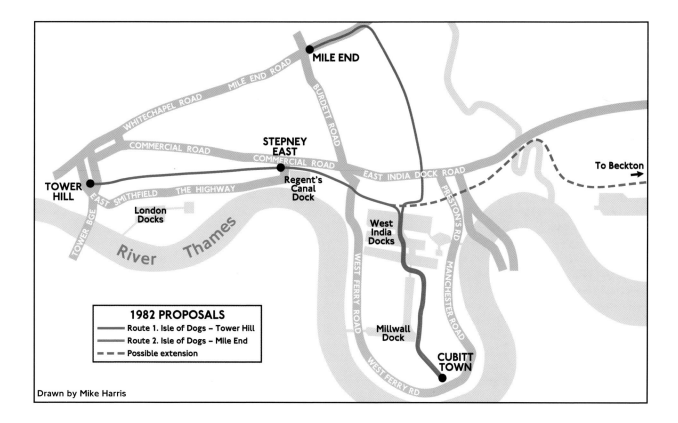

1982 PROPOSALS
— Route 1. Isle of Dogs – Tower Hill
— Route 2. Isle of Dogs – Mile End
- - - Possible extension

Drawn by Mike Harris

The 'central' route was more or less what materialised into today's DLR, crossing the West India Docks from north to south, with a station planned at Canary Wharf. On this location, the report says '... if extensive dock filling takes place, this could provide a good location. Otherwise it would be very isolated with poor traffic prospects'. Extension across Millwall Outer Dock to Cubitt Town did not feature in this proposal and the terminus was to be sited at Tiller Road. However, in its manifestation as the DLR, the 'central' route turned east before reaching Millwall to adopt the southern part of the 'western' alignment, crossing Manchester Road to terminate at Island Gardens.

The north–south route had originally been put forward as a fall-back option to provide a basic rail connection into Docklands if the direct east–west option proved to be too expensive. However, in the light of the LDDC population and employment forecasts, and in the absence of any direct connection to the south of the river, it became clear that the north–south route was needed as well as and not instead of east–west. For the north–south line, a street tramway was also a possibility, with trams running from near Mile End Station along Burdett Road to Limehouse, East India Dock Road, and then onto West India Dock Road, from which point the north–south route would move onto segregated track to share whatever alignment was eventually selected for the east–west line on the Isle of Dogs.

With both these outline schemes, there remained scope for extension at a later stage off the east side of the Isle of Dogs towards the Royal Docks and Beckton, where stage 2 of the Docklands regeneration programme was planned.

A final report, jointly prepared by the GLC, LDDC, the government and LT, was issued in June 1982 recommending the construction of two light rail lines comprising a 'west–south' route from the City to the Isle of Dogs, and a 'north–south' route from Mile End Station to the Isle of Dogs. Within three months, government funding was promised for the Docklands Light Railway.

Somewhat unusually, funding was authorised before a Parliamentary Bill had been deposited. This was provided by the Department of Transport and the Department of the Environment jointly, on the strict understanding that the total of £77m not be exceeded and that the project be completed by 1987. Funding came with a remit to take full advantage of existing technology, yet to avoid technical solutions which might compromise the target cost or opening date, or compromise reliable and economic operation. Furthermore, the completed railway was to be operationally self-sufficient, with no revenue support promised by government.

Initial Royal Assent was granted in April 1984, the delay being partly caused by the 1983 General Election, and partly by an unresolved Parliamentary petition during passage of the Bill through the House of Lords.

In the meantime, a very significant alteration was made to plans for the Mile End section of the second route. The climate was not yet right for the Highway Authority to accept street running along part of the very busy A11, Mile End Road. This proved to be convenient for the LDDC which was keen to see a high-tech automated system in place, and this could only be possible if the entire route were to be fully segregated. This desire also over-rode proposals which considered using the wide Burdett Road from Mile End to Limehouse, a much less busy thoroughfare than the Mile End Road, which could have met with the approval of the London Borough of Tower Hamlets, especially if a segregated crossing of the Commercial Road could have been created at Limehouse.

The alternative alignment took the line further north along the railway cutting beyond Bow before climbing steeply and suddenly eastwards to parallel the main East Anglia railway on embankment to terminate instead at a disused bay platform at Stratford Station. The DLR would therefore not serve Mile End, although the interchange facilities with other modes afforded at Stratford were undoubtedly more comprehensive, and it was actually a better traffic objective in its own right than Mile End would have been. A second DLR Bill reflected this change before being deposited in November 1983, with Royal Assent granted in April 1985.

The original intention was to invite tenders based on engineers' designs and specification in the time honoured way, and place one contract for mechanical and electrical engineering, and another for civil engineering works.

A report from *The Times* dated 23 August 1984 announcing the contract for DLR placed the previous day.

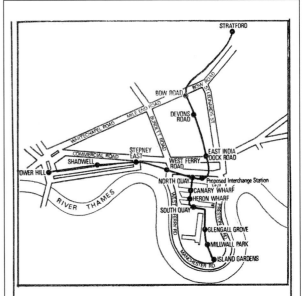

Route of the Docklands railway (top) and an artist's impression of the train.

£60m driverless railway contract for Docklands

By Our Transport Editor

Britain will get its first driverless passenger trains in 1987, on London's new Docklands Light Railway.

But the lightweight trains, carrying up to 1,500 passengers an hour each way between Tower Hill in the City and Docklands, will have a person on board to check tickets, help passengers, and start the train in stations.

A £60m contract for the railway was awarded by London Regional Transport yesterday to a consortium of GEC and John Mowlem against fierce international competition. The contract includes construction of 7½ miles of track from Tower Hill to the Isle of Dogs and Stratford; 11 two-car automatic trains; 16 stations; and signalling, maintenance, and control equipment.

Following direction from government in mid-1984, it was decided to invite tenders for a single design and construct contract for the entire railway, with tenderers free to offer equivalent alternatives to the basic specification.

In August 1984, a contract was placed with GEC-Mowlem. Now that the railway was to utilise a fully segregated alignment, the automatic train operation that came as part of their package could be accepted.

Until the era of the large-scale development proposals for the Isle of Dogs (from mid-1986 onwards), the DLR was expected to actually have to look for traffic and customers, rather than, as has happened since, to at times have an embarrassment of business. Thus, the planning assumed relatively low hourly figures to move – 1,500 initially, per hour per direction. This capacity level resulted in a planned timetable of eight departures per hour on each of the two legs of the initial Railway, combining to give a more impressive 16 trains per hour serving the combined section of route on the Isle of Dogs. It was to meet this part of the Performance Specification that the tendering parties bid in 1984 and it was this simple timetable that the railway used for its pre-marketing. However, what had seemed attractive, and indeed almost too good to be true to some local residents in 1984, proved to be inadequate by the time the railway was ready to carry passengers a mere three years later.

Planning work to upgrade the system began before the public opening in 1987. Simply put, the planners required the railway to be rebuilt with a remodelled main junction at Poplar and with longer platforms to accept two-unit trains.

A full size mock-up of the interior of a car was built to gather views of the layout before finalising it.

Below The London Borough of Lewisham began campaigning for an extension to Lewisham in 1987. The DLR reached it in 1999.

The trains were to be run more frequently with an improved signalling system and with more operational flexibility provided by reversing facilities at Crossharbour and a passing loop at Pudding Mill Lane. The railway company at the same time was required to run a passenger service to meet the expectations of the growing workforce and the local residents who had long been promised better public transport.

£50m dock rail extension south 'could bring 25,000 jobs'

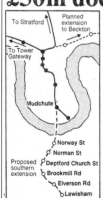

By John Spicer

A £50 million extension of the Dockland Light Railway under the Thames into south-east London could bring 25,000 job opportunities to people living in the surrounding suburbs, according to two local authorities.

Officials argue that such a link would alleviate peak hour road, rail and Underground congestion and would cut journey times into the City and docklands development area.

The proposal has been put forward by the London boroughs of Lewisham and Greenwich, after an economic and financial evaluation of a dockland railway extension commissioned by the two authorities.

Officials now have to con-

vince London Regional Transport that theirs is the best of several ideas being considered to improve travel links south of the river.

Launching the report yesterday, planners from both authorities said the two-mile extension would run from Mudchute on the Isle of Dogs, through a single-track 850-yard tunnel under the Thames, then a double track rail to Lewisham.

It would have six stations and would be capable of carrying 10,000 passengers in the morning peak period, equivalent of 15 million passengers a year.

The estimated capital cost of the scheme ranges between £34.6 million and £52.4 million at March 1986 prices.

The authorities say the disparity is because of the difficulties in assessing future land values.

They say the Government, London Regional Transport, the dockland development authorities and business, with some money from themselves, would finance the project.

The study underlined the high unemployment rates on both sides of the river, saying boroughs north and south would benefit considerably. Greenwich, which attracts 1.25 million tourists a year, had huge potential to create further employment in tourist-related jobs, the study says.

Mr Terry Scott, chairman of Lewisham's planning committee, said the proposed route of the extension would mean

minimal disruption to housing. Alignment along the banks of Deptford creek and the river Ravensbourne were technically feasible, leaving only about 12 houses affected.

He said London Regional Transport regarded the scheme as a "front runner" and one of the most sensible they could undertake.

The study says that if the extension is built there would be 2,400 fewer people travelling into London on the Underground or British Rail and 3,000 fewer in the buses.

It would reduce the demand for commuter parking and "rat-running" in Greenwich and Lewisham from increased traffic generated by docklands development.

The report says that inner

London residents had seen the decay of many of their shopping streets while retail developments were going on in outer London. That was creating a "doughnut" effect with new investment being concentrated around the M25.

The proposed railway extension could help to attract the private sector to provide an additional 2,000 jobs in Lewisham centre.

The proposed extension is supported by the London Planning Advisory Committee.

Dockland Light Railway Extension to Greenwich/Lewisham: Economic and Financial Evaluation by Halcrow Fox and Associates (London borough of Lewisham, Town Hall Chambers, Rushey Green, Catford, London SE6 4RY; £5).

Crossharbour in 1987, with the station in the background and work on construction of the siding in the foreground.

Building the DLR

Although it may seem that the DLR was blessed with being able to use a lot of redundant railway land that no-one else had previously claimed, it was still necessary to establish relations with a great number of parties before construction could begin. In particular there were more than one hundred tenants trading from arches underneath the old viaduct on the City area; at certain other places, notably south of Bow Church Station and between Mud-chute and Island Gardens other very sensitive property and occupation matters had to be tackled. Two-thirds of the 7.5 route miles (12.1 km) of the 1987 opening railway uses former disused or under-used railway. Some considerable new works, in volume and variety, were necessary to accommodate the DLR.

Starting at the City end, the original terminus at Tower Gateway is constructed on a reinforced concrete viaduct. A double track viaduct, since modified and rebuilt for the Bank extension, had been constructed eastwards parallel to the BR-owned Fenchurch Street lines. In this area a reinforced concrete slab supported by the existing viaduct and independent foundations was constructed. Elsewhere an independent steel and concrete composite design has been used. At Cannon Street Road (1 km east of Tower Gateway) the DLR joined the BR viaduct and adopted two original BR running rails.

At Shadwell the BR viaduct was used to carry the island platform structure. A 200 metre reinforced concrete viaduct was constructed south of Limehouse Station (then called Stepney East) to avoid the existing BR running lines and to link into the western end of the disused brick arch viaduct of the former London & Blackwall Railway. From here to near to the north side of the West India Docks, the line used the 1839 constructed viaduct, a Grade II listed structure.

No fewer than 11 wrought iron bridge decks needed replacing with new concrete decks, although the old side girders were put back in to retain appearances. At West India Dock Road the two-span bridge was reconstructed to incorporate the original solid pink granite columns in the road. As originally built, the line rose up on to a standard steel and concrete composite structure leading to North Quay junction, originally built with 40-metre radius turnouts as part of three double junctions. South of this junction the Docks Crossing began. Specially fabricated 65-metre spans were provided in each of the three docks with an 8-metre clearance over the water of the dock. This structure, which in the mid-1980s dominated the skyline, soon became dwarfed by the vast office buildings around it. South of the West India Dock system, the line turns east on a 50-metre radius curve and then winds its way south through the island on standard elevated structure although a specially fabricated section was used to cross the Millwall Cut, the stretch of water connecting the West India and Millwall docks.

South of Crossharbour station the line used an earth embankment before being carried on a new viaduct containing Mudchute station to join the 27 surviving arches of the single track Millwall Park viaduct. This part is now disused.

The route from North Quay junction to Poplar and Stratford was built with several one-off features. The bridge over what was the Docklands Northern Relief Road, now Aspen Way, is a 50-metre span skew plate girder bridge. Poplar Station was originally built on retained-fill immediately southwest of the Operations and Maintenance Centre. The old trackbed was re-ballasted and new drainage provided north of Poplar. A steel plate girder bridge was needed to cross the Limehouse Cut Canal south of Devons Road because the earlier structure had decayed badly.

North of Bow the Bow Curve takes the line from the old cutting to run beside British Rail on an embankment featuring a 1 in 25 gradient on a 100-metre radius curve. New ballasted track was laid towards Stratford on the alignment of the most southerly of the BR lines and only minimal engineering work was needed to adapt the western end bay platform for DLR trains to use.

The Initial Railway had been constructed under a design and build contract with GEC-Mowlem Railway Group carrying out all the tasks necessary to provide a complete railway. This formula was repeated with the extension further into the City, to Bank Station. On 17th July 1987 – before the original railway had even opened for traffic – two contracts were awarded; to Edmund Nuttall Ltd for the westward extension in tunnel to Bank, including construction of the DLR station at Bank; and to GEC-Mowlem Railway Group for the upgrading of the existing system, extension of electrical systems through the E. Nuttall contract works, and provision of new vehicles.

The original Island Gardens Station on DLR was built on viaduct and is seen here under construction with test running already taking place.

A single 100-tonne tunnelling machine was constructed in Britain, to a German design, to bore the tunnel part of the 1.6 km extension westwards from Royal Mint Street. Following a Start of Tunnelling ceremony on 14th March 1988 the westbound tunnel was bored first, breaking through into the new King William Street station site on 7th December 1988. The machine was then withdrawn from the westbound tunnel and put to work digging the second one, to become the eastbound tunnel. This bore was completed in February 1990. Tunnelling through the London clay was achieved at an average rate of nearly 100 metres per week.

The circular cross section tunnels were bored by the 5.39 metre diameter tunnelling machine, then lined with precast concrete segmental lining: the internal tunnel diameter is five metres. This tunnel diameter permits the provision of a walkway on one side, which allows not only access for maintenance but evacuation of passengers, including mobility-impaired passengers, in an emergency. In order to bore the seven-metre station tunnels the existing tunnelling machine was plugged into the centre of a larger 7.75 metre station tunnel machine, retaining the smaller

machine's facilities to power the larger machine. As much as 200,000 tonnes of clay was excavated and taken to various sites east of London including the site of the former Beckton Gasworks. Generally, the tunnels were bored at depths greater than 30 metres below ground with the Bank Station at a depth up to 42 metres below ground.

Besides the tunnelling carried out by machine, ventilation shafts, access points, escalator shafts and interconnecting tunnels were dug by the traditional hand method. In order to minimise surface impact, available space on street corners was used for worksites: as well as the main contract site at Royal Mint Street beside the DLR, four other worksites were used at Fish Street Hill, Lombard Street, Lothbury and Bucklersbury.

As well as the main work, substantial effort was needed to rebuild and integrate the London Underground station to provide links to the new DLR facilities. In particular a new concrete slab was cast above the existing station to support a new building to be constructed over the ticket hall. This required 30 metres deep hand-dug shafts to accommodate the necessary vertical piles.

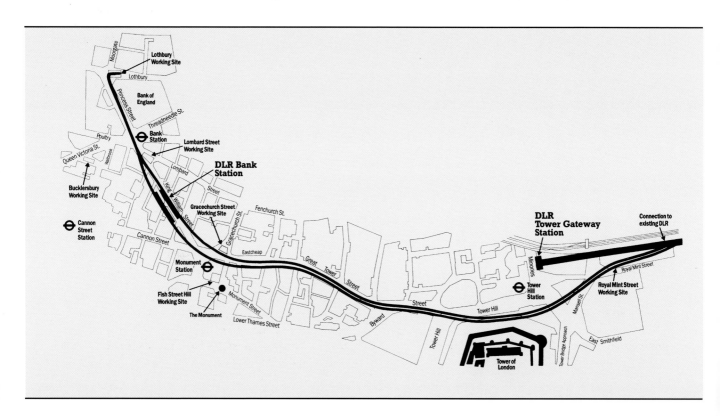

At the same time as the decision-making process gave the go-ahead for the physical extension of the railway to Bank, a decision was taken to upgrade the rest of the railway to handle more passengers.

The upgrading work divided into five main parts: the strengthening of structures, where necessary, to run two-unit trains; lengthening platforms to handle these longer trains; infrastructure improvements to aid operational flexibility; buying more trains; and specific upgrading work such as the total rebuilding of Canary Wharf Station.

It may seem difficult to appreciate now, but until the advent of the Canary Wharf scheme for the Isle of Dogs it was intended that the main DLR service would be from the City to Beckton with the Isle of Dogs to be served by the north–south service from Stratford, passengers changing at Poplar between one route and the other.

The main Beckton contract consisted of approximately one-third each of elevated, ground level and trough or underpass-level railway. Concrete structures which are more expensive but more substantial then the earlier steel/concrete composite design are used throughout for the elevated portions, which are located principally in the Poplar to Leamouth/Brunswick areas, at the Connaught Crossing viaduct and near Gallions Reach station.

Where the DLR crosses the River Lea a post-tensioned box girder bridge with a 74-metre span has been erected. Further east, the track descends to ground level but two stations, Beckton Park and Cyprus, were constructed in the centre of the Royal Albert Dock spine road as part of that contract. The track is also located within an underpass near the eastern end of the route in order to pass under the Eastern Gateway access road which is the main link road to the A406 North Circular Road.

Resulting from the enormous creation of employment in Docklands it was soon realised that the area immediately south of the Thames needed a good connection with Canary Wharf, but the DLR could not be extended to other administrative areas using LDDC channelled finance. Lewisham borough had initially proposed the extension to Lewisham and was actively supported by Greenwich in feasibility, route and environmental studies. A Parliamentary Bill was deposited in November 1991 and received Royal Assent in May 1993.

There were to be no major problems to overcome, but by virtue of the need to tunnel under the Thames and to provide a viaduct to align the project into a practical entry to Lewisham it could not be low cost. Under Government help and direction a significantly new private finance initiative was set up. This produced the full designs for a financeable scheme but showed that the cost of the river crossing would prevent a positive return to the investors. Thus private and public partnership was developed to provide the £50M difference in finance from a number of state and local sources. To enable DLR to manage the provision of the extension it has been organised as a concession granted to a new railway and at the end of the concession all the property and assets will be transferred to DLR. This new railway attracted seven consortia to bid for the contract, and the winning group under the name City Greenwich Lewisham Rail Link PLC (CGLR) was responsible for producing the railway and will maintain the infrastructure for 25½ years, which includes the construction phase. CGLR receives an availability fee from the opening date up to year 2009 and from then on a usage fee tied to passenger numbers. In return CGLR must make the whole extension available to year 2021 for the DLR train service operator to run the service required of it. The result has brought 500,000 more people within 45 minutes travelling time of the Docklands area. Journey times of 30 minutes from Lewisham to Bank or Stratford and 16 minutes to Canary Wharf are now on offer. Service intervals vary between 4 and 10 minutes for the different times of day and days of the week and correspond with the intervals north of the river.

The Lewisham extension joined the existing railway north of Mudchute station, with a replacement station built north of the original Mudchute stop. It then goes underground on the north side of the old Millwall Park alignment with a new sub-surface Island Gardens station constructed north of the original terminus station, which was demolished. The tunnels go under the River Thames with an underground station, called Cutty Sark, built between Thames Street and Creek Road in central Greenwich.

The line then curves south-westwards to surface near the existing Greenwich station, continuing as an elevated railway along the alignment of Deptford Creek. A station has been built at Deptford Bridge with the route then continuing principally through existing open space towards a stop at Elverson Road, proceeding to the west of Conington Road to terminate at a station south of the National Rail Lewisham station ticket hall. The DLR terminus at Lewisham is partly below ground as the site is not flat.

The Woolwich route of DLR is being constructed in two distinct stages with the opening of stage 1 as far as King George V being already achieved in December 2005. This

The stock yard of tunnel linings for the Woolwich extension, as viewed from King George V station.

Above right Viaduct construction in progress, with the assembly machine holding a viaduct section over a pier close to Silvertown Road.

Below right The first train movement on the new extension took place for gauging purposes in August 2005. West Silvertown station is in the background.

serves the major traffic centre of London City Airport. The second phase is the authorised extension to Woolwich Arsenal which was commenced in August 2005. Much of the first phase has been constructed on viaduct built by an Italian consortium utilising a giant building machine. All the concrete sections of the viaduct were cast locally at Thames Wharf in a temporary building. The reinforcing framework was assembled and welded first and the mould assembled around the reinforcing for concrete casting. This provided a controlled environment for quality production alongside the line. The transportation then to site being very short. The building machine travelled on the completed track-bed and bridged the section to the next pier allowing it to lift the prefabricated concrete sections into place and hold them during assembly.

The completed viaduct is a box section for strength and low weight with the track deck on top. The adjustable framework made it possible to steer the machine for all the viaduct alignments. As each span is completed the machine can advance along to bridge the next section ready for assembling that section. The construction in the Thames Wharf area is mostly embankment except for a short viaduct to enable a station to be constructed with development of that site in the future.

The phase 2 of construction will take the line from the temporary terminus at King George V where the track level is just below the surrounding ground into a cutting to the under river tunnel portals. These tunnels will be bored individually and similar to the Lewisham tunnels.

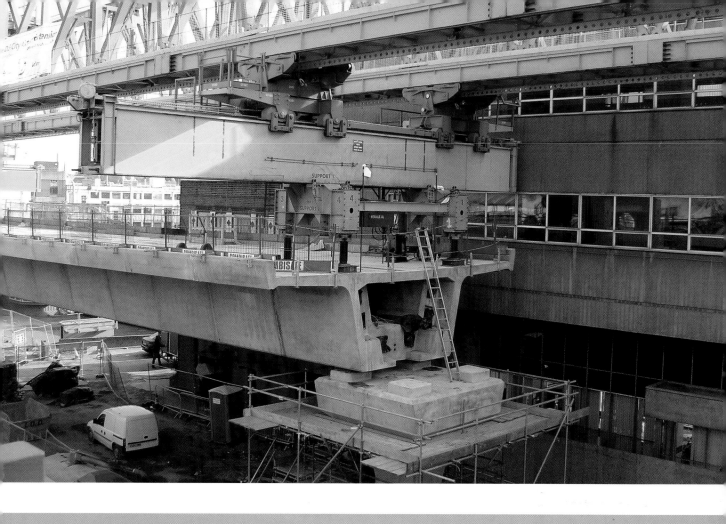

The Routes Described

Within DLR the routes of the railway are referred to both by geographical direction and by terminal station. The line maps no longer use different colours for the services operated on DLR as the operation is represented on the Transport for London maps with a petrol blue colour line. The present line maps have each service as a distinct line from terminal to terminal to allow passengers to understand how to use the DLR.

When DLR opened there were only two services: Tower Gateway to Island Gardens using the West and South Legs and Stratford to Island Gardens using the North and South Legs. In 1991 the West Leg was extended to Bank and in 1994 the East Leg to Beckton opened. The South Leg was extended to Lewisham in 1999 with a new line to King George V and serving the London City Airport opening in December 2005, identified as the South-East Leg.

Opposite The international welcoming signage at Tower Gateway terminus opposite the Tower of London.

Above Tube tunnelling methods were used for the underground platforms at Bank.

The West Leg or Bank Route

The West Leg was originally taken to Tower Gateway as its terminal in the City of London. Before actual opening the project to go to Bank for a western terminal was under way. Bank Station on DLR is below all the London Underground platforms here and has two side-platform tunnels bored either side of a central concourse tunnel that provides access from either end to the other Underground lines using Bank.

The line runs eastwards in twin 5 metre diameter bored tunnels generally under the streets and rises at a gradient as steep as 6% to a sub-surface portal east of Mansell Street. The line continues east at 6% gradient rising to a junction with the original line from Tower Gateway above and to the north of Royal Mint Street after which the junction is named. The line to Bank has become more important than the original line to Tower Gateway but the latter has been kept to allow diversions as well as for Beckton trains.

In March 2006 the Duke of Edinburgh paid a visit to the DLR as part of a visit to Greenwich, starting his journey at Tower Gateway. Tower Gateway terminus was governed by space constraints and has a narrow platform and two tracks.

The Tower Gateway terminus was built close to the eastern end of the National Rail Fenchurch Street terminal. This is close by the London Underground station at Tower Hill which is a designated interchange. The DLR station is on the eastern side of the street called Minories and is equipped with a platform level concourse accessed by escalators and having small retail facilities. The two stations are linked by public subway and street crossing. The platform continues directly from the concourse and is a single narrow island with two tracks and a full length glazed canopy supported on columns centrally placed. A subsidiary entrance is available at the eastern end.

The line eastwards is on new structures until Cannon Street Road where the National Rail services are reduced to two tracks allowing DLR to take the original viaduct space relinquished in 1985.

The line now is on the oldest structures in the DLR network dating from 1840 as part of the London and Blackwall rope-hauled operation. The next station at Shadwell is an island structure east of Watney Street. This now has a full length glazed canopy supported centrally along the platform. It was built to the west of the original L&B station as that had too little space for the new station platforms. Shadwell is adjacent to the East London line station of the same name.

The old viaduct is used as far east as Butcher Row

The listed viaduct at Limehouse.

where a new viaduct alongside the National Rail tracks leads directly to Limehouse Station. This station provides an interchange with services out of Fenchurch Street station and significant interchange occurs in rush hours. To cater for the passenger numbers the platforms are equipped with large gull-wing glazed canopies that are braced together across the tracks and thus offer good protection from weather.

East of this station DLR runs on the route of the London and Blackwall railway that was not widened and was abandoned by British Railways in 1962. Its two tracks carry DLR past the Regents Canal Dock where the first signs of the considerable re-development of Docklands are observed. The dock is also called Limehouse Basin and has modern residential buildings alongside and a main road tunnel below. The River Thames is seen close by to the south with the connecting river lock in view. The line con-

tinues past the remains of the original Limehouse Station and close by the new flats of Narrow Street with the spectacular developments of Canary Wharf in view rising out of the old sailing ship docks of the Isle of Dogs.

Westferry Station has also been upgraded to have full length glazed canopies with gull wing design and braced across the tracks to cater for the many passengers interchanging between DLR services here.

East of Westferry Station the junctions known collectively as North Quay Junctions begin. The tracks continue directly east wards towards Poplar Station to become the East Leg of DLR. Tracks also diverge to rise up and turn south to take trains on to the South leg. The viaducts are an amalgam of the original L&B and modern concrete of the new DLR. The DLR viaducts are the originals from 1987 with additional sections from the upgrading to achieve four tracks at West India Quay.

Westferry Station is one of those modernised since opening with better shelter for passengers.

All Saints Station with an enlarged version of the original shelter design. Devons Road (right) and Bow Church have been similarly updated. At Devons Road there has been new housing development next to the station (below right).

The North Leg or Stratford Route

The North Leg of DLR starts in North Quay junctions immediately north of West India Quay Station. It firstly is taken eastwards through the central tracks of Poplar Station which also serves to interchange passengers with the East and South East Legs. This eastwards section passes the connection into Poplar Depot and immediately turns northwards on to the old alignment of the former North London Railway and soon reaches All Saints Station, which serves the busy East India Dock Road and Crisp Street Market.

The line is then in cutting and heads north on gently rising gradient to cross the Limehouse Cut canal into Devons Road Station, serving the older residential area in this location. From Devons Road northwards the line continues in

cutting, passing under the tunnel formed by a sheltered housing complex, into Bow Church Station. This serves the busy Bow Road area and is an interchange to the London Underground District Line via a 300m street walk. These three North Leg stations are provided with full-length canopies of the original styling from 1987 of semicircular glazed design. These are the last of the design which was created to be the major common feature of the stations as originally built in 1987.

The North Leg of DLR then has to climb from the cutting station at Bow Church on to the embankment alignment of the Great Eastern Railway to continue towards Stratford Station terminus. This is accomplished by a single track curve climbing on to the south side of the embankment and by the single track taken over from National Rail to a formerly disused bay at Stratford.

Above The platforms and street level building at Bow Church.

Right North of this station the railway becomes single track.

After the railway opened the need to improve service on the North Leg was achieved by installing a passing loop at Pudding Mill Lane laid out to have a station built later. In 1998 this station was opened as an island platform.

The terminus at Stratford using the existing structure has been outgrown by the passenger loadings and a new terminus is under construction with two elevated tracks and platforms located south of the Central line and over the Jubilee line area.

Stratford station offers good interchange to services of National Rail and London Underground. In the next phase of DLR expansion the platforms of the North London Line will also see DLR trains.

A passing loop was provided at Pudding Mill Lane and a station was added later. Lack of space prevents the complete stretch of line between Bow Church and Stratford being double-tracked, but a new terminus is being built.

Canary Wharf is the largest and most impressive station on DLR.

The South Leg or Lewisham Route

The South Leg was in the original DLR of 1987 and built across the areas of the West India and Millwall Docks that had been taken out of use and were scheduled for development. Its original terminal was an elevated station at Island Gardens.

The start place for the South Leg to Lewisham is West India Quay station, which is directly at the south end of the North Quay Junctions. This has been greatly extended from the original two-track side platform arrangement into a four-track with two island platforms design. This arrangement is to allow the adjacent junction to have a significantly greater capacity with only the southbound

Lewisham trains conflicting with the northbound trains to Stratford. This station serves the new hotel and residential buildings on the North Quay of the West India Docks as well as the revitalised and restored sugar warehouse of 1802. The remaining conflicting junction is to be removed to allow extension of train length.

Continuing the very short distance across the dock on four tracks, the line enters the grand overall roofed station of Canary Wharf located between the high commercial buildings which now dominate this location. The expected passenger numbers here are catered for by providing three tracks each having two platforms. The four tracks from West India Quay converge into the three tracks for Canary Wharf, so allowing the centre track to be used as a major

Above The glazed roof of Canary Wharf station.

Right The recently enlarged station at Heron Quays.

reversing point for services. All platforms are accessible by escalators and stairs from ground level and the side platforms also connect directly into the retail facilities on either side on that level.

Continuing southwards the three tracks converge into two to cross the middle dock to the substantial Heron Quays Station. This station straddles the original 1987 viaduct and the platforms form part of the commercial development structure beside and over the railway. The developments on Heron Quays include a subsurface retail mall. Escalators are provided for the large numbers of passengers the station is designed to accommodate. It is an alternative interchange for the Jubilee line.

South Quay Station is of unique design on the DLR and was built to replace a structure damaged by an IRA bomb attack.

Continuing southwards the railway bridges the south dock and swings sharply eastwards on the original 1987 alignment and proceeds to South Quay Station. This station is the third on the site and was built in 1996 to replace the bomb damaged second design. It will be closed completely when the capacity improvement to three vehicle trains is completed as the track curvature makes it impossible to have longer platforms. A new station over the adjacent Millwall Cut waterway will be built to replace it.

The railway continues eastwards over Millwall Cut waterway and turns south around a curved commercial building built after the railway and along to Crossharbour station. This has facilities like Westferry and Limehouse with platform canopies cross-braced over the track. It is used for terminating trains when required as it has a centre pocket siding immediately to the south. Crossharbour Station serves some commercial buildings and the district centre supermarket. There is also a considerable residential

community now in the nearby area which is expected to continue growing.

Moving further south the railway passes over a scissors cross-over and past an emergency siding to begin its descent to the under-river crossing. It next reaches Mudchute station which is in shallow cutting adjacent to the tunnel portal. This location is in complete contrast to the original line here which was built on modern viaduct. The station name is explained by the location of the huge dump of dredged mud from the docks laid through a shute and now grassed over.

All of the original DLR line here has been erased with the exception of the listed brick section viaduct of the North Greenwich line which opened in 1872 and first closed in 1926. The newer line opened in 1999 and provides cut and cover parallel single-tracked tunnels to the new Island Gardens Station, a centre island design situated just below ground level.

A train enters Mudchute Station, before taking the under-river connection to Greenwich and Lewisham.

Between Mudchute and Elverson Road this style of passenger shelter is used at the open-air stations.

From here southwards are the bored tunnels under the river with their steep descent past the sump level and which then rise to Cutty Sark Station. This station serves Maritime Greenwich and being very close to the river is deep underground with two escalators to the surface. It is built in a cut and cover box and includes a traction supply sub-station on the intermediate floor level. This station does not have provision for extension to three-vehicle train operation and will require special treatment.

Continuing southwards the line is still in bored tunnels and climbs towards Greenwich National Rail station passing through the rectangular chambers where the tunnel boring machines were removed and into cut and cover section twin tunnels. This quickly changes to a double tracked section under the old station platform and rises to the DLR platforms on land originally having the 1835 London and Greenwich Railway tracks. Greenwich DLR station is integral with National Rail facilities, with cross platform connections convenient for journeys from South East London to Canary Wharf. Turn back facilities are provided here by a scissors crossover.

The route is then taken onwards by a twisting viaduct largely located over the River Ravensbourne and its tidal section of Deptford Creek to an elevated station named Deptford Bridge constructed over the main A2 roadway.

The valley of the River Ravensbourne then provides a direct way towards Elverson Road station which serves northern parts of Lewisham. From Elverson Road there is a short section on to the Lewisham terminus located at ground level within the angle formed by the two National Rail embankments. The DLR station thus lies in the approaches to the older facility, making very convenient interchange. It has a central platform that leads directly out to the roadway opposite the shopping centre.

This page Island Gardens Station entrance at street level and a view of the platforms in box tunnel just below.

Right Lewisham Station is located in the centre of National Rail facilities with good bus connections.

Above Poplar Station and the neighbouring depot. The DLR Control Centre is located in a separate purpose–built building housing both the control room and the necessary equipment rooms and training facilities.

Right East of Poplar Station is the elevated section of the Beckton route. At ground level is a Stratford train. Blackwall is the first station on the elevated section.

The East Leg or Beckton Route

The East Leg directly continues from the West Leg at the North Quay junctions area and passes through the outer tracks and platforms of Poplar Station. This station is the operational hub of the railway with the depot facilities adjacent. The line moves eastwards and either side of the North Leg tracks to climb on to the viaduct taking it past Blackwall and East India Stations. These serve the developments both commercial and residential of the former East India Docks.

The viaduct continues on a sweeping curve bridging over the Lower Lea Crossing road complex and the curves of Bow Creek waterway where the River Lea approaches the Thames. The line enters the wild life sanctuary now created on the creek banks and makes a tight curving approach to Canning Town Station complex. The DLR forms the upper level of the station directly over the Jubilee Line and with National Rail North London Line tracks to the east. This major station is a significant interchange point for rail and bus services and lies parallel to the Silvertown Way road viaduct.

The East Leg continues on past a turn-back siding and to the junction for the Airport line to the south east and turns under Silvertown Way through Royal Victoria Station to Custom House Station. This is the main station for the giant exhibition centre of ExCel which creates significant traffic for DLR.

Beyond Custom House the station of Prince Regent leads on to another long viaduct, first passing over the Connaught Crossing road over the Royal Docks and into Royal Albert Station. Eastwards from Royal Albert Station is the dual carriageway of the Royal Albert Docks Spine Road within which the DLR tracks are located. The stations of Beckton Park and Cyprus are at ground level within the elevated roadway roundabouts and are known as bowl stations.

Above One of two stations for ExCel is at Custom House.

Above right Prince Regent Station serves both the east end of the ExCel exhibition halls and new hotel facilities at Connaught.

Right Connaught crossing, with recently built hotels in the background.

From Cyprus the line curves first south and then north and rises to an elevated station at Gallions Reach which serves the developing land to the east of the Royal Docks that was once the Beckton gasworks. Within this area is the DLR Beckton depot where most vehicle maintenance is performed. The tracks continue north and drop to ground level under the approaches to the planned East London River bridge over the Thames and make a curve to finish facing westwards at the terminus station at Beckton. The station serves major residential areas and the District Centre supermarket.

Top The descent to one of the bowl stations on the Beckton branch.

Above Platform level view of the bowl station at Beckton Park with the road roundabout above.

Right Beckton depot, the main stabling and maintenance facility on DLR. The cleared land to the left of the depot will accommodate an exension to the facilities in readiness for the next generation of trains.

The South-East Leg or King George V Route

The South East Leg is the newest route of DLR and its area of service is south of the Royal Docks which takes in the London City Airport. It is to continue on into the Woolwich Arsenal extension to be opened 2008/2009. The line starts from south of Canning Town Station on the East Leg. There is a section of viaduct for provision to construct a station at Thames Wharf before continuing on embankment and viaduct to West Silvertown Station. The line then passes through Pontoon Dock Station before the viaduct curves around to allow it to approach the major elevated station structure close by the London City Airport terminal building. Connection from the centre island platform into the airport is available by escalator to ground level. The line continues east past the airport terminal and car parking to descend a ramp to the King George V Station in North Woolwich. This station is the temporary terminus, having a central island slightly below local ground level to facilitate the descending approach to the tunnel that will take the route under the river to Woolwich Arsenal.

Above West Silvertown Station platforms.

Above right West Silvertown Station exterior

Right West Silvertown Station is in the distance in this view of the elevated section of the DLR which comprises most of the City Airport extension.

Above London City Airport Station interior looking towards the airport tunnel.

Left Train approaching London City Airport from King George V with a refurbished vehicle and one from the batch built in 2001.

Above right King George V platform immediately after opening.

Right The start of the Woolwich Extension at King George V.

DLR trains

On any railway, the trains present the most important element of a passenger's journey. It is now generally recognised that a train is not solely a functional piece of hardware, but an essential part of the image, both in external appearance and the internal finish and comfort. This was realised by the railway's joint clients and by the contractor, and substantial efforts were made to ensure high standards of engineering and finish.

In the context of the DLR in its initial form, evolving a whole new design for just 11 vehicles could not be justified. Main contractor GEC-Mowlem therefore co-operated with Linke Hofmann Busch (LHB), one of Germany's main builders of light railway vehicles. The eleven vehicles of what became known as 'P86' stock, were delivered by road and sea via Hamburg and King's Lynn from August 1986, the first (01) arriving at Poplar on 7th August of that year.

Opposite A train of refurbished B92 stock stands at Canary Wharf.

Above This side view of an eastbound train leaving Westferry shows externally hung sliding doors and the blue stripe which now adorns all refurbished DLR trains, referring to its close proximity to the River Thames.

The last vehicle of the first batch, No. 11, was to make history several times. It was delivered direct to Manchester on 9th February 1987 as the key part of a light rail demonstration there and became the first revenue-earning DLR vehicle. The vehicle was temporarily modified to accept a pantograph for the overhead power collection system installed by Balfour Beatty, a conversion which was remarkably simple involving little more that an additional roof member and a length of conduit to carry the main power cables down to its underframe. Vehicle 11 was thus the last to be delivered to the DLR at Poplar on 30th March 1987. In the hands of Train Captain Gary Bonini, No. 11 carried Her Majesty the Queen and His Royal Highness the Duke of Edinburgh from Island Gardens to Poplar, and thence to Tower Gateway, on the occasion of the Royal Opening of the railway on 30th July 1987. Vehicle 11 was also the first to be despatched to its new owners in Essen, Germany, on 14th November 1991.

There were 84 seats in each car, mostly arranged in transverse bays of four to take full advantage of the large windows offering fine rooftop views of the changing Dock-lands scene. To increase circulation space, 12 longitudinal seats were provided in the centre section of the train, along with two wheelchair bays. The railway has some regular wheelchair users, but the bays are most heavily used by shoppers with wheeled trolleys and baby buggies, taking advantage of the railway's superb roll-on/roll-off facilities. In order to achieve good access for unassisted wheelchair users, the cars were designed to have a level car floor to platform gap of only 75mm. This led to the adoption of inward-opening ('bat wing') swing plug doors. These were never an ideal solution but, with the traffic levels forecast at the time the contract was awarded, it was anticipated that the layout would be acceptable.

However, the enormous upturn in development on the Isle of Dogs put this aspect in a different perspective.

The initial fleet of eleven vehicles was supplemented by a further ten – the P89 stock – to increase the capacity of the Initial Railway and for the first phase of services underground to Bank. These were very similar to the first (P86) batch with only detailed modifications – mostly under the skin – made in the light of operational experience, the need for longer (two-vehicle) trains, and to enable them to operate underground to Bank. P86 trains were prohibited for underground running, as they did not meet tunnel running safety requirements.

Other differences included new illuminated destination displays and the fitting of bulbous panels by the (inward) opening doors in an attempt to discourage passengers from standing in that area (a feature that was also added to the P86 trains). Blue-tinted fluorescent lights were also provided at the 'driving' ends to reduce reflection for Train Captains when driving manually in the darkened conditions.

The additional ten trains were ordered as part of the upgrading contract in July 1987 and differed from the initial vehicles in that they were constructed in the UK. During 1986 BREL decided to enter the light rail market and entered a co-operative agreement with LHB, whose products are largely complementary to those of the UK builder. The DLR trains were the first products of this development, being sub-contracted by the GEC-Mowlem Railway Group to BREL, York. Numbered in the series 12–21, the first vehicle was delivered by road, arriving at Poplar on 12 December 1989, the last one on 4 May 1990. After commissioning and trials, the first to enter service did so on 11 May 1990.

It was originally envisaged that the P89 stock would provide the stock required for the Bank extension, but the unprecedented increases in passenger traffic and the authorised extension to Beckton highlighted the need for even more trains, and the capability to operate double length (two-vehicle) trains wherever possible. A contract was subsequently awarded to BN Constructions Ferrovaires et Metalliques of Bruges in Belgium, initially for ten more trains of what became known as the B90 stock. This would have given a total of 31 vehicles in the DLR fleet (11 x P86, 10 x P89 and 10 x B90), but the BN order was increased to 21 vehicles (11 x P86, 10 x P89 and 21 x B90 – total 42). A mock-up of the new B stock was made available for public inspection in late September and early October 1989, by which time the requirement for additional stock from BN had grown to 44 trains.

The B stock has sliding doors, provided to improve boarding and alighting at stations, necessary because of the far greater use of the DLR than was originally envisaged. These doors, outside-mounted, form part of the loading gauge and the width of the main vehicle body is thus fractionally less than the P stock. There are also fewer transverse seats, allowing a greater standing capacity within the train. A front opening door allows access between coupled units. This was really superfluous because, apart from in emergency situations, there are no footplates over the couplers between vehicles, and in the Bank tunnels, in an emergency, access and detrainment is via the side doors onto specially provided side tunnel platform walkways. The front seats for forward viewing remain, however, although the emergency driving console for the Train Captain has had to be 'split' into two sections, one on each side of the front door. The door operating panel for the Train Captain is located down the left hand side of the double doorway positions, rather than over the doorways as on the P stock and conventionally upholstered seats replace inset moquette panels used hitherto. All of the electronic equipment is located in a single locked interior cabinet.

The final order for B stock comprised 70 trains, divided into two sub types – 23 of B90 stock and 47 of B92 stock. The first train of B90 stock arrived via Dartford Docks at Poplar on 31 January 1991 and was available for test running and crew training from 23 April. The last vehicle arrived on 27 September. The first train to enter service did so on 1 July 1991. These trains, like the P89 stock, are able to operate singly or two coupled together, but the two types were not initially compatible. 'Light Rail' roundels were to be fitted to B90 trains, but only 14 received them because of the impending announcement that the DLR would be taken over by the London Docklands Development Corporation from 1 April 1992.

One train was fitted from the start with Alcatel equipment for testing purposes – a section of track in the Poplar area was set aside for trial and test running from 9 September 1991. Joining this train later were two Alcatel-equipped B92 trains to give three vehicles for testing.

Because of the ever-increasing numbers of passengers using the DLR, especially the Bank branch in the peaks, measures for increased vehicle capacity were undertaken. The result was an internal rearrangement of one train, where additional standing space was created but at the expense of 20 seats throughout the vehicle, or ten per centre bay. Grab rails replaced grab handles and much extra standing room was available in the door area. Whilst successful in its way, a modified design which enabled greater standing room was subsequently agreed upon, with a total of 20 B92 vehicles to be so converted, completed by the end of March 1999.

There was sufficient rolling stock to provide the service on the Lewisham extension, which opened on 22 November 1999. However, there was insufficient stock for any future extension or expansion and with the extension to London City Airport expected to be given the go-ahead, a further 24 vehicles were ordered from BN in Belgium and were delivered over 12 months from January 2002. They are almost identical (and are completely compatible) with their predecessors, but cosmetic changes include white painted exterior passenger doors, dot matrix destination displays, and a completely new design of seating moquette. They entered service between June 2002 and March 2003, supplementing the existing fleet of B90 and B92 stock, making a total of 94 vehicles.

These extra trains, known as B2K stock (although collectively, the fleet of 94 vehicles is regarded as B92 stock) also gave the opportunity to refurbish the earlier trains and Alstom of Wolverton were awarded the contract. The refurbished trains are compatible with non-refurbished vehicles, the changes being mostly of a cosmetic nature. The refurbished trains sport a bright red livery with a wide blue 'swirl' (representing the railway's close proximity to the River Thames) and grey doors. Each vehicle also has a small side dot-matrix destination display. Inside the vehicles, the seating layout has been revised with more transverse seating and the interior grab rails are in light green.

Interior view of a refurbished B92 stock vehicle looking towards the articulated section.

Details of DLR B stock can be summarised as follows:

Length:	28m
Length over coupler:	28.8m
Width over doors:	2.65m
Body width:	2.50m
Overall height:	3.468m
Weight:	36 tonnes approx (tare)
Seating capacity:	70 (12 transverse pairs, 42 longitudinal, 4 tip-up)
Total capacity:	284 (6 passengers/sq m)
Maximum speed:	80km/h (50mph)
Bogies:	2 BN monomotor bogies, 1 BN trailer bogie
Traction:	Brush Electrical Machines
ATO/ATP:	Westinghouse (ATO), GEC (ATP) for 22 trains, Alcatel of Canada for 48 trains (as delivered to DLR). The first 22 trains have since been converted to Alcatel.
Wheels:	Resilient wheels of 740mm diameter new, 660mm min
Min track curve:	38m

The B90 stock, although equipped for operating with the original GEC signalling system, was easily converted to Alcatel in readiness for system-wide operation. To that end, the first vehicle was withdrawn for conversion on 29 October 1993, re-entering service with its B92 counterparts on the Beckton branch opening day, 28 March 1994. Conversion of the other B90 vehicles followed, the last being completed in April 1998.

Following the derailment of vehicle 45 between West India Quay and Canary Wharf on 21 October 1995, it returned to service on 6 November 1995 in a trial 'Corporate livery' of petrol blue. This actually comprised adhesive material over the old colours. In this, it remained unique until given an all-over-advert livery in November 1998, the experimental livery never being adopted. All-over advert liveries also played a significant part, with a number of different schemes carried from then until 2005, including four vehicles painted specially in a 'Back the Bid' livery, promoting London as the City to host the 2012 Olympic Games.

The first batch of DLR stock – the P86 – was not allowed to carry passengers on the Bank extension, as it was not designed with the necessary safety features for tunnel operation. Further, extensive conversion would be necessary to enable operation on the new Alcatel signalling system. Options considered included 'upgrading' the trains to make them suitable for tunnel work, to scrap them, or to find a buyer. In fact all eleven trains were purchased by Essen Verkehrs AG of Essen in 1991 for further service and with their new owners were fitted with pantographs and cabs. The first vehicle to leave the DLR for its new owner did so on 14 November 1991. Others gradually followed, the last in December 1995.

In the meantime, consideration was given to replacing the 'bat wing' doors on the P89 stock, to make access easier. Coincidentally, two P89 vehicles were involved in a collision at West India Quay delta junction on 22 April 1991. BREL at Derby were awarded the contract to repair the damaged portions and also to do the alterations to the passenger doors – this train was thus the ideal prototype. It was decided that single-leaf doors would replace the inward folding doors, but because the vehicles were built to the maximum loading gauge, they could not be fitted outside the body shell as on the new B stock. Therefore the doors had to slide back into specially constructed pockets which meant some interior seating alterations. No seats were lost, but the transverse pair by the draught screen at each new pocket position was turned to become longitudinal. Door controls by the door sides as on B stock were fitted, as were door-close warbler tones. The bulbous panels by the doors were removed as they were no longer needed. The repaired and converted train arrived back at Poplar on 18 December 1991, re-entering service in its new form on 27 February 1992. Conversion work on all ten vehicles was completed by August 1992.

Although the P89 stock was able to operate over the whole of the Initial Railway, including the underground section to Bank, extensive upgrading work would have been required for it to work on the Alcatel system. All ten vehicles were thus withdrawn on 7 July 1995, the last day of the GEC signalling system. As with the P86 stock, three options were available for the P89s and in the end the decision was taken to sell these ten vehicles to Essen too. Between December 1996 and August 1997, the ten vehicles were gradually transferred to Essen.

The continued expansion of the Docklands Light Railway, with a further extension from King George V to Woolwich Arsenal, the takeover of the North London Line to serve Stratford International, and three-vehicle trains on the busiest routes, led to an order for 24 new trains from Bombardier in April 2005. They will be built in Germany at

The design of the 24 trains ordered for 2007/08 delivery.

Bautzen. Electrical equipment will come from Mannheim and the bogies from Siegen. They will be delivered between May 2007 and September 2008.

With the DLR already being well established and the very high level of integration and automation, the new fleet must be very similar to the 94 operating vehicles. Thus this new fleet will quite closely follow the present vehicles in size and shape. The contract has fixed the internal layout to be the same as that for the present fleet post-refurbishment. The external shape will have some differences around the ends to cut down the angularity. Air secondary suspension will be used to ensure floor level is maintained with different loads and the passenger load can be also measured to allow traction and service braking forces to be adjusted to follow the load.

The main changes are with the electrical equipment and the contract includes the provision of three-phase motors and the control using now-proven Insulated Gate Bipolar Transistor (IGBT) converters. The bogies will thus be significantly different and will have one motor per driven axle. There will be four driven axles on the two outer bogies with a non-driven articulation bogie. The equipment in the contract has been in use on various other European operations already. Although the doors will appear to the public to be similar – but with glass panels descending much further than on the present stock – the real difference will be electric operation instead of air. Whilst the rest of the design will be much the same as now, there will be little interchangeability of parts with the 1990 design. The auxiliary electrical equipment will be powered from an IGBT converter/inverter with the heavy loads supplied at 400 Volts three phase.

The contract called for two variants of design to be submitted based on whether or not electrical coupling with the present B92 vehicles was provided. Mechanical coupling was mandated to allow rescue to be performed with the older vehicles. The Bombardier offer using a new internal wiring structure was accepted with no electrical inter-coupling. The use of trains that cannot have different vehicle types inter-coupled was agreed as acceptable operationally. The new vehicles will use the present maintenance facility.

Station design

The initial railway had to be constructed to a strict, frugal budget which was achieved using a virtually standard kit of parts from which most stations could be provided. All stations required platforms raised up 1000mm above rail head so that the vehicle floor nominally maintained at 1025mm is only slightly above the platform. All platforms were initially provided with a canopy area less than the full length of the platform, a semicircular arch continuously glazed with polycarbonate panels. With a semicircular shape a high degree of self cleaning is achieved. This arch was light and airy but provided good cover for waiting passengers. It was generally arranged to be adjacent to the

entrance steps and these were positioned according to the restrictions of each site. All the platform train indicator and public address equipment was fixed in the canopy. Since the back and end walls surrounding most platforms were provided from a kit assembly of panels that had fixing places on the top of each upright it was easy to fix a canopy or lighting columns as needed along the platform. For the original railway most stations have side platforms but the original Poplar had centre islands forming four platform faces, with both Tower Gateway and Shadwell having a single centre island. These island platforms required the arch roof canopy to be mounted on central columns. An original station completely different from the others is Stratford because it used an already existing but unused platform of the existing much bigger station. The standard DLR equipment had to be fitted around the existing canopy supports and the ticket machine was included in the wall of the equipment room to keep all the facilities together and preserve the one platform solely for DLR. Some additional canopy provision was made later since the expansion to two vehicle trains forced many passengers to endure poor weather without any protection for a time.

Almost as soon as the railway opened in 1987 the work to extend stations had to start, and for the simple side platform arrangement this was easy to achieve. The big contrast was between the original but never opened Canary Wharf and the huge and dramatic complex that serves the centre of commerce now built around the old dock wharfs.

The only new station provided along with the upgrading of the original stations was at Bank. This bored tunnel station being at rail level 42 metres below street was designed to be the new major connection of DLR into the City of London and since the Bank Station complex was already a major transport hub the DLR was slotted in as another layer below all the others. DLR facilities at platform level are the same as elsewhere and a control room is provided to manage passengers' needs.

Towards the end of the 1990s many of the original stations received considerable improvement in the passenger environment. Various extensions to, or complete replacements of, canopy roofs were carried out. The more heavily used west leg and south leg stations with side platforms have been fitted with an overall roof, glazed over both platforms but not in the centre over the track. The island platforms at Shadwell and Tower Gateway have a new grander version of the original canopy which extends the full platform length. The north leg intermediate stations have lower traffic levels and the canopy improvements installed have been based on extending the existing design, using new units, to provide cover along the whole of the platform.

The need for a second generation of stations resulted from the Beckton Extension and its place in the regeneration of the Royal Docks area. The original railway had grown in provision of station capacity as passengers from the huge developments of the older docks swarmed onto the platforms. The extensions had to be tailored into the old with a less than integrated visual result; anything else would have needed closing sections for more drastic change. With the Beckton Extension the opportunity arrived to provide a newer design to fulfil the capacity need now perceived for the stations. The completely new flying junctions west of Poplar allowed Poplar to be provided with four platforms, thus forcing the complete rebuilding of track and station.

The station facilities are the same as for the upgraded original stations but the station architecture is very different. The canopies are not an arch but more like a gull wing when viewed along their length and cover about half the two-vehicle length of each platform. The canopy is completely glazed in flat glass sheets. The support structure consists of round columns from which alarm boxes and signage are mounted. The platform train indicators, loudspeakers and lighting are suspended from the glazing bars to give the impression of openness in design. There is minimal difference in layout between side or island platforms. All platform surrounds and access ways are fitted with fully glazed panels for complete feeling of light and openness. This also gives no hiding place for troublemakers, thus giving passengers perception of lower risk to themselves. The lift towers are also much more prominent in that they have illuminated panels on top in red to act as a more visible sign for the station.

The extension to Lewisham was achieved as a project controlled and specified under the needs of financial return on investment for the concession holder City Greenwich and Lewisham Railway (CGLR). The open-air stations fall into the same design needs as the majority of stations built earlier. Those stations underground are box-section cut and cover rather than tube.

The main difference at above ground stations is in the design of the canopies. For lower maintenance there are only short canopy sections and these have metal panelled roofs rather than glazed ones. Each platform has two separate sections of canopy.

Both underground stations have an island platform and although the basic equipment is the same the individual design is very different. Island Gardens, being close to the surface, has the southern part open to the sky and access is by stairs. Cutty Sark is 20 metres below the surface at track level and has two mezzanine levels and escalators. Lifts for the mobility impaired are provided at both, in common with the rest of the system.

The platforms at the rebuilt Heron Quays feature a light display. The adjacent Canary Wharf developments and service upgrading necessitated replacement of the original station.

Below Heron Quays Station at ground level.

Cutty Sark Station upper mezzanine floor with the tunnel boring machine faceplate set into the wall to show passengers how the tunnels were dug.

Below A new station is planned at Langdon Park between All Saints and Devons Road on the service to Stratford.

The Train Service

The initial 1987 peak service called for 9 trains operating at 10-minute intervals on each route, and 7 trains in the off-peak every 12 minutes. An enhanced peak service using 10 trains was introduced later in 1988, with intervals of 7½ minutes scheduled on each service. At the same time, the station dwell times were reduced. The off-peak service was also increased to every 10 minutes (9 trains).

With the upgrading of the Initial Railway commencing very soon after its public opening, it became necessary to close down certain sections of the line for engineering work involved and to run buses in place of the trains. This started in May 1988, affecting all routes after 21.30 daily, with sections of closures at weekends prior to 21.30. However, from 11 February 1989 it was decided to close the entire railway at weekends as well as from 21.30 on Mondays to Fridays and this remained the case for several years. There were certain exceptions to this to meet special events.

Above The formal opening of the City Airport extension.

A train in original livery (left) at Mudchute, with a refurbished train.

Entry into service of the P89 stock allowed a modest service increase from 5 November 1990, with 13 single-vehicle trains being scheduled. This saw the peak service improved to 6½minute intervals necessitating the regular use of the passing loop at Pudding Mill Lane (between Bow Church and Stratford and then without a station).

From 25 February 1991, following a long period of testing, two-vehicle trains were timetabled for the first time. The timetable saw the peak-hour services on both branches increased to 5-minute intervals with seven two-vehicle and eight one-vehicle trains scheduled on the Tower Gateway to Crossharbour and Stratford to Island Gardens services respectively. This was the first regular use of the new Crossharbour centre reversing siding, where all the two-vehicle trains had to reverse, as Mudchute and Island Gardens could then still only accommodate one-vehicle trains.

The first stage of the opening to Bank took place on 29 July 1991 when the Tower Gateway peak service was halved, and alternate trains diverted to operate to and from Bank, which also had a 10-minute service. Trains running to and from Bank used the westbound tunnel on a 'single line' basis. By now many two-vehicle trains were able to be operated of both P89 and B90 stock (but not of mixed types), and the peak stock requirement was for 7x2 (Bank/Tower Gateway to Crossharbour) and 8x1 (Stratford to Island Gardens). In the off peak period, each service operated every 10 minutes (Bank, Tower Gateway and Stratford).

The completion of the eastbound running tunnel and subsequent full opening of the Bank extension on 29 November 1991 called for a total of eight two-vehicle trains in the peaks, four each on the Tower and Bank services. Total stock requirement was thus 8x2 and 8x1, 16 trains and 24 vehicles. (The proposal to run a five-minute peak service to Bank and no service at peak times to Tower Gateway was dropped at a late stage, and certainly after publicity had been made available announcing the proposal). The off-peak service was the same as hitherto, with the Tower Gateway service operated by single vehicle trains and extended to Island Gardens.

Although major upgrading work had been proceeding on the Docklands Light Railway from very soon after its opening, Mudchute and Islands Gardens stations on the south leg still remained capable of accommodating one-vehicle trains only, a problem being the restricted space at Island Gardens and the possibility of a future extension under the River Thames to Lewisham, which would need new stations anyway. However, it was subsequently decided to lengthen these two stations to take two-vehicle trains and the quickest option was to close completely for a period of time from after traffic on Friday 6 March 1992. Because of the restricted space available at Island Gardens, it was only possible to lengthen one platform (No.2), the other being retained for single-vehicle trains only.

The timetable introduced on Monday 9 March 1992 changed operating patterns and train formations considerably. This was the first use, on a regular basis, of the centre platforms at Canary Wharf for reversing purposes (where Stratford trains terminated), with Bank trains (two-vehicle) and Tower Gateway (one-vehicle) terminating at Crossharbour. With each service operating at eight-minute intervals, this called for 9x2-vehicle and 6x1-vehicle trains – 15 trains, 24 vehicles. This increased the capacity on the Stratford branch, with a two-vehicle train every eight minutes (peaks) instead of a one-vehicle train every five minutes. Both Bank and Tower Gateway gained more frequent services (every eight instead of ten minutes).

The railway south of Crossharbour re-opened on Sunday 12 April 1992, but because of uncompleted work, two-vehicle trains could still not operate to Island Gardens until 8 June 1992. With the restoration of through services, the principles of the previous timetable continued. Requiring one extra vehicle (10x2 and 5x1) throughout the day – 15 trains, 25 vehicles – the eight-minute pattern on each service continued.

Until the original sections of the DLR were connected to Alcatel signalling, the Beckton service, from its opening on 28 March 1994, comprised a self-contained shuttle service operating from 05.20 to 21.30 on Mondays to Fridays. Between 07.00 and 19.00, five two-vehicle trains provided a 10-minute service and outside these times three trains operated a 13-minute interval service.

The increasing use of the new offices around Canary Wharf saw continued increases in ridership, especially on the Bank branch. A six-minute peak service was introduced between Bank and Island Gardens from 31 May 1994 with marginal reductions on the Tower Gateway – Crossharbour service.

After several years' absence, from 3 October 1994 late-evening services were resumed on the Initial Railway network, operating until around 00.30. The Beckton to Poplar shuttle continued to finish at 21.30.

The Bank service was further increased to 5-minute intervals in the peaks from 9 January 1995, which enabled the Tower Gateway and Stratford services to revert to even 10-minute interval services. This saw an increase in stock required to 21 trains and 38 vehicles.

Saturday services resumed after a gap of over six years from 20 May 1995 but only between Tower Gateway and Island Gardens and between Stratford and Canary Wharf. Saturday services began around 06.00, which was half an hour later than on Mondays to Fridays, as a result of the additional time required for the computers to changeover from the old to the new system. A similar service pattern on Sundays began on 25 June 1995, operating between 07.30 and 23.30. Meanwhile, the whole railway changed over to the new Alcatel signalling from 10 July 1995, with services continuing to operate on existing schedules. (It was not until December 2001 that Saturday services started 30 minutes earlier at Monday to Friday times and Sundays at 07.00 instead of 07.30).

Bank station gained a Saturday service from 29 July 1995, while on Mondays to Fridays from 31 July 1995, the Beckton service was extended to Tower Gateway. This meant that for most of the day, this terminus served two routes – Island Gardens/Crossharbour and Beckton. The peak service required 22 trains and 38 vehicles. For the first time, the Beckton branch had a service after 21.30, which also operated through to Tower Gateway. During this late-evening period, the Tower Gateway to Island Gardens service was discontinued, the latter destination being served by trains from Bank.

The continuing increase in the numbers of passengers using Bank station in the peaks resulted in alternate Tower Gateway to Crossharbour trains being diverted to Bank as a stop-gap measure from 30 October 1995. This reduced the service to Tower Gateway to every 20 minutes, although it was still served by the Beckton service. This meant that Bank had one additional train (five instead of four) in each 20-minute period. The stock requirement remained unchanged.

Weekend changes saw an all-day Tower Gateway to Beckton service introduced from Saturday 16 December 1995 and from the following day, Bank received a Sunday service for the first time.

Further increased services on the DLR would be dependent on the reconstruction of the West India Quay delta junction. Trains used the new junction from 27 December 1995, but on existing schedules. From 22 April 1996, enhanced peak services were introduced. Bank had a 4-minute service but because the single line section to Island Gardens could not accommodate such a frequent service, the service beyond Crossharbour was halved to every 8

minutes. The peak-hour Stratford and Beckton services were each improved to 8-minute intervals, while the Tower Gateway to Canary Wharf service operated every 16 minutes. This service required 26 trains and 44 vehicles. From 6 January 1997, however, the peak service between Tower Gateway and Canary Wharf was eliminated which resulted in 23 all two-vehicle trains required for service.

Peak services were increased further from 26 August 1997 with services based on a 7-minute pattern, enabling Bank to have a 3½minute peak service. Tower Gateway continued to be served only by Beckton trains in the peak, comprising a mix of single and double vehicles. The stock requirement was thus increased to 28 trains and 52 vehicles.

With the morning peak being more concentrated than the evening, services were enhanced yet again from 20 April 1998, but in the mornings only. Bank was given a 3-minute peak service, Stratford 6 minutes, while Tower Gateway to Beckton was marginally reduced from 7 to 7½ minutes. This service called for 30 trains and 56 vehicles in service during the morning peak, but the stock requirement for the evening peak remained unaltered. The morning peak requirement for 56 vehicles (out of a fleet total of 70) proved a little optimistic and the Bank to Crossharbour morning peak service was cut back to terminate at Canary Wharf from 1 September 1998. Whilst morning peak services remained based on the 3/6-minute principle (6-9 minutes Tower Gateway to Beckton), the stock requirement became the same as for the evening peak – 28 trains, 52 vehicles.

The closure of the line south of Crossharbour for reconstruction work for the Lewisham extension saw minor changes to service from 11 January 1999. The same service patterns applied in each peak, but in the evening the Bank to Crossharbour service was cut back to Canary Wharf. This was to enable the reversing siding at Crossharbour to accommodate a reversing Stratford train and a reversing Bank train (that would have previously gone on to Island Gardens) every 7 minutes. All trains were scheduled to be formed of two vehicles, the morning peak requiring 27 trains (54 vehicles) and the evening peak 25 trains (50 vehicles).

Test running between Crossharbour and Lewisham began on 22 August 1999 with certain trains from Bank and Stratford being extended (empty) over the new extension. Service patterns remained unchanged over the 'public' sections of the network.

Full passenger services to Lewisham began on 20 November 1999 and the opportunity was taken to standardise both peak services. Of course, even more trains were required for service, stretching the 70-strong fleet to the limit. The new timetable required 30 trains (60 vehicles) in both peaks. The evening peak was reduced by two trains from 30 May 2000 because the passenger demand is concentrated over a longer period than in the morning.

The first stage of applying a 'Metro' type of service at the extremes of the day on the Docklands Light Railway began on Mondays to Fridays from 18 February 2002, when late evening service intervals were improved on all routes to 10 minutes – a 10-minute interval service is the minimum requirement for a turn-up-and-go service. This principle was introduced at weekends from 24 August 2002 and on every day of the week, a 10-minute service was provided on each service, viz -

- Bank – Lewisham
- Stratford – Canary Wharf
- Tower Gateway – Beckton

Although there is always some 'tweaking' of the service to match provision with demand, the maximum number of trains for peak service remained unchanged until the additional B2K trains became available in 2002, when peak services were enhanced from 27 August. 35 trains (70 vehicles) were required for the morning peak service and 30 trains (60 vehicles) for the evening peak. This remained the case until the extension to King George V (serving the London City Airport) opened on 2 December 2005, when further increases were implemented.

The current Monday to Friday services on the Docklands Light Railway can be summarised as follows:

Service	Morning Peak		Evening Peak	
Bank – Lewisham	3½	18x2	4	16x2
Stratford – Crossharbour	21	2x2	8	6x2
Stratford – Lewisham	7-14	6x2	-	-
Tower Gateway – Beckton	7	9x2	8	9x2
Bank – King George V	14	4x2	16	4x2
Canning Town – King George V	14	2x2	16	2x2
Trains in Service:		41x2		37x2

Service	Midday		Evening	
Bank – Lewisham	10	6x2	10	6x2
Bank – Canary Wharf	10	3x2	-	-
Stratford – Lewisham	10	6x2	-	-
Stratford – Canary Wharf	-	-	10	3x2
Tower Gateway – Beckton	10	6x2	10	6x2
Bank – King George V	10	6x2	10	6x2
Trains in Service:		27x2		21x2

Bank is served by five trains every 14 minutes in the morning peak and five trains every 16 minutes in the evening peak, with four going to Lewisham and one to King George V. To double the service to King George V in the peaks, a shuttle is provided at the same intervals to and from Canning Town. The Saturday 'busy' (08.30 to 19.30) and Sunday 'busy' services (10.30 to 19.30) require 26 trains (52 vehicles).

Major Capacity Improvement

Major capacity improvement will be needed by 2008 on the Bank to Lewisham service to cater for the growth of passenger numbers. Other services will then need such improvement soon afterwards. The Stratford service has had work started first as the single platform terminus with its narrow platform is a major constraint on the service pattern of the whole railway. In early 2005 a contract for the design and building of a new Stratford terminus was let and this will be built to the south of the present Underground Central line tracks on a viaduct over the Jubilee line circulating area. This will remain a DLR terminus when the station is renamed with the opening in 2007 of the nearby International station. For the DLR approach to the International station see the section on approved extensions, page 60.

This new Stratford station will allow for three vehicle trains but the other stations on the north route of DLR will not immediately be given extended platforms. Capacity improvement becomes available with the ability to operate twice as many two vehicle trains as with the original layout.

For Bank to Lewisham it is necessary to lengthen platforms and in many cases this will be done using the provision already designed in. At some stations it is already available, with the latest rebuilding at Heron Quays also giving the required platform length. The biggest problem is South Quay station which cannot be extended on the present site. Thus a completely new station is to be built along the viaduct over the Millwall Cut, which is straight enough although has significant vertical curvature.

For the stations on the Lewisham extension there are a number of problems in extending platforms. At Lewisham itself, whilst there is apparent space it is important to ensure that more than half of the new longer platform is outside the short tunnel under the National Rail tracks. This has to be achieved to ensure the station is not reclassified as underground and thus require continuous staffing for safety reasons. The present end of track, being at road level, cannot be extended to allow the greater over-run buffer distance needed.

The biggest problem is with Cutty Sark station where the station box is deep underground and only two vehicles long. The cost of extending the platform tunnels is not acceptable against the revenue predicted for the station with longer trains. The solution postulated at time of writing is to dock each train with the leading half vehicle and trailing half vehicle still in the tunnel just off the platform. The station will be fitted with apparatus to tell the train not to allow door release for the half vehicles not at the platform. All vehicles will need to be fitted with the necessary receiver to prevent door release. Each vehicle would require this at each end. If a failure did allow door release in the tunnel, the side walkway would prevent any significant danger to passengers. This is considered acceptable as the vehicles and the Alcatel signalling cannot cost-effectively be changed to provide this function just for one station. Adequate notices will also be fitted to tunnels at Cutty Sark.

The next problem is Tower Gateway. This station normally serves the Beckton branch but also has to be used when access to Bank is not available. The fitting of three vehicle trains into the present space has been judged unsafe as the platform width is too narrow for the passenger numbers. The present layout of an island structure cannot remain therefore and the station has to be reduced to one platform on the site of the present platform 1. The platform extension will be on a gradient. The track will be altered to provide a passing loop to give capacity for two trains to be off the main line to Bank.

To enable three-vehicle trains stabled in Poplar depot to enter or leave service at Poplar station the platforms there will be extended concurrently with the main route.

The City Airport extension to King George V has been built with three-vehicle length platforms but this service is operated to Bank with two-vehicle trains until demand makes it viable to change.

Running slightly fewer three-vehicle trains rather than the maximum number of two-vehicle trains provides better stability of operation. The railway signalling is already available for operating three-vehicle length trains.

Signalling and Train Control

The original schemes for the building of the DLR had contained elements of street tramway running. The eventual scheme that went forward to construction achieved full separation from the highway and thus automatic operation could be invited from bidders. The desire of DLR was that tried and tested systems would be used. The successful contracting group provided a system of signalling based on the then very successful British Railways Solid State Interlocking system. Instead of visible signals for manual driving, the system provided audio frequency tones fed to the rails and to an inductive loop system laid between the rails. These tones provided the safety information for the over-riding protection system and the basis for instructing the train to move, which was carried out by an on board micro-computer that had a stored profile of the whole railway. Each station was equipped with a data link to and from the train to ensure each train was maintained with correct information and to perform supervision. This formed a station-to-station fixed block system adequate for the initial railway with its small fleet of trains and low service frequencies anticipated. Much of this was implemented with equipment already in use on other metro or suburban rail operations.

Almost immediately after opening, upgrading of the system was started, having been already specified for the Bank tunnel extension. This maintained the same system components and achieved capacity increases by reduction in block lengths with its consequent considerable increase in track mounted equipment. The upgrading also extended possible train length to two vehicle trains.

On top of the safety signalling was an extensive Automatic Train Supervision facility that was developed from an existing American computer-based system already adapted to light rail control in Buffalo New York State.

The Railway soon attracted a significantly higher patronage than originally planned for and as soon as late 1989 and into early 1990 a performance specification was assembled for contractors to bid for a full resignalling. The specification allowed any proven system to be tendered with upgrades. No significantly new proposal would be considered. A competition between traditional fixed block, with many additions, against an existing transmission based moving block system resulted, and the moving block proposal was chosen as it potentially offered a higher capacity of working. The ability of a transmission based system to accept change with much lower need to make physical changes to lineside equipment offered much easier integration of the expansions to the Railway already in the pipeline.

Thus in May 1990 the Alcatel company from its Canadian SEL division received a contract to re-signal the railway and was given the benefit of providing the original equipment of the Beckton branch as a test track. The Alcatel product had already been significantly demonstrated with the system in use at Vancouver in Canada since 1986 following a long development and proving period.

The Alcatel system is centred on the product called SELTRAC which consists of a triple redundant safety programmed central control communicating very frequently with all the vehicles in the controlled area. These vehicles may be coupled into trains when any train has one vehicle selected to be in charge. Each vehicle has a duplicated safety programmed computer system which reports position and takes movement instructions safely. Moving block is created from dividing all the track into positions each of approximately 6.25 metres length and having the vehicles report back, to this accuracy, of their positions. The system takes into account all the circumstances surrounding each train and instructs the vehicle controlling each train what it should do. As a result the trains can run closer together and the capacity of the railway can be increased. With a train of several vehicles, those vehicles not in charge are available to be in charge should this be necessary.

Another system advantage with this is full bi-directional running on all tracks. This is available always and the guideway listings held in the control centre include all facilities needed to run full service in either direction, restricted only by the track layout. The normal running is left hand, but right hand running can be used for maintaining service in the event of an obstruction or other special circumstance.

The communication with the train is performed using the inductive linking between the cable loop laid on the track and the antenna coils mounted under each vehicle. This allows a frequency current flowing in the track loop to produce a voltage in the train receiving antenna. The train transmit antenna will also induce a current in the track loop for the return information. Both paths use different sets of frequencies to ensure both security and non-interference. The messages are also timed on a basis of each vehicle being polled and a return message sent back. Only one message at any time is being passed through.

The whole system is based on knowing where the train is, first by detecting it at fixed places and then calculating the movement from the vehicle reports. This is primarily achieved by dividing the track into individual inductive loops. These vary in length and on DLR the longest are about 2km and the shortest a few hundred metres. Each loop has its own unique address which the train can recognise and respond to. The cable is laid on the track and crosses over the two conductors every 25 metres. This helps in electrical noise reduction and provides a positive signal phase change to be seen by the train. The train counts these phase changes along the loop as the next measure of position along a loop. The train is equipped with wheel rotation measuring detection of 110 pulses per revolution. So the train can calculate its position very finely and report to the Control Centre an adequate 6.25m accuracy. This report is a digital code which the control centre system can compare with its own position data tables and get a fix for each train from its frequent reports.

Unlike the original provision for the railway which put a lot of computer held intelligence into each vehicle, the transmission based moving block puts much more into the control centre instead. The whole geographic track information is held centrally. To ensure this computer data is correct, extensive testing is performed to ensure accuracy for all parameters before public service is allowed.

SELTRAC functions by instructing each train in the controlled area as to the limits of its movement in such a way that the train believes it is constantly approaching, or is on a braking curve to, a target stopping point on the track. This braking curve is being advanced along the track whilst the train is required to accelerate or maintain speed. When the train is required to brake, the target point ceases to be advanced and each successive message will have a shorter distance to go to the place where the train should stop. With a station stop there has to be more information given to the train to enable the braking curve to end accurately

with a train position within the tolerance for safe door release. This has to include not only the accurate place along the track but which side of the train the door release is given. This must take account of which way round the controlling vehicle is on the track. Each vehicle has an A end leading or a B end leading but its Vehicle On Board Controller (VOBC) is located in the B end. This makes the side to release instruction dependent on the end leading.

To ensure that the train is actually operating within the controlling instructions, the controlling vehicle creates the braking curve it has been instructed to follow from the given stopping place ahead and the brake rate it should control to. This is actually three curves since no automatic train control system can achieve exact control. The three curves represent a desired state, an upper limit for that desired state and the emergency brake triggering state. The controlling VOBC emergency brakes the train if the safe envelope is breached at any time.

As each vehicle is initially available for use to control the train, only one actually has to remain available. This offers true redundancy, unlike any system needing the leading vehicle to be in charge in more conventional ATO/ATP. The Alcatel system provision for DLR was contracted from the beginning to be able to handle three vehicle trains. Clearly if the actual station is not yet able to accommodate this, the door release conditions cannot be given and the central system has these removed to avoid an unsafe situation. In 2005 approval was obtained to invest in all the station and structural additions needed to start three-vehicle train service on the Bank to Lewisham service in 2008. The only system change will be incorporating the train stopping positions. The complications with short trains can be resolved as necessary within this.

To allow for the safe detection and protection of any train that becomes un-tracked, there has to be an interconnected back-up system that can ensure train detection in these cases. To enable this to be achieved without direct electrical connections with the rails a system using axle counters is employed. This is arranged generally as a fairly course station to station traditional signalling block section system. Additional axle counter blocks provide local point locking facilities. Axle counters which work on inductive detection and phase reversal principles are widely used on traditional signalling, particularly in mainland Europe. The detector heads send pulse information to the Axle Counter Evaluators which are located in trackside equipment rooms. On DLR points are locked locally to ensure movements of trains under full manual control are

safe with no central system functioning. All these facilities are incorporated into a Station Controller facility which communicates with the Central Control system.

For the depot at Poplar on the original railway no automatic operation was provided. The original main line system was not suitable for the confines of a depot where very short block sections are needed and each siding can have trains berthed very close together. This made driving manually the only solution and the trains already had this mode and a very restricted speed. The use of low speeds made simple two-aspect colour-light block signalling an affordable system. To ensure the driver of a train was given clear routeing there was also a route indicator when any diverging points where in the route. To reduce the installation costs for a system that essentially did not need to be fully fail-safe it was implemented with simple jointed 50Hz track circuits and used industrial programmable logic controllers for the logic and the control panel driving.

With the resignalling in 1994 there was an option to provide automatic depot control for the new Beckton depot and to retrofit Poplar depot. This option was not taken so Beckton was constructed with the same programmable logic control and the track circuiting done with switched audio frequency circuits. These were again implemented with jointed track because of the very short block lengths.

Extending the number of vehicles in the fleet in 2002 required some extra track to be fitted into Beckton depot in the places for which passive provision was already included. Thus all the 94 vehicles could be fitted into Poplar and Beckton. This is a difficult operation with sidings not designed for multiple two vehicle trains and will be worse with three vehicle trains in the future.

To enable more trains again to be stored and to make more trackage suitable for three vehicle trains, Beckton depot has been expanded to achieve the 2007 delivery of new vehicles. This new layout will include a full turning loop to ensure both parts of the depot can have access both ends.

Track

The track used on DLR is standard gauge of 1435mm. No gauge widening is used for the many low radius curves. The minimum radius used for depots and emergency cross-overs is 40m but this is not used for normal service mainline track. The minimum used main line is 50m and that is now restricted to parts of the original railway, principally on the South route. Track construction uses a mixture of methods. Track substantially on ground level or on viaduct that has not got special requirements is mounted on sleepers mostly of concrete type but in some places timber has been used. The original railway concrete slab viaducts have track mounted on a concrete track slab cast over the main viaduct taking up all the differences of tolerance in construction. The later concrete viaducts for Beckton are made as a trough with ballast and conventional track. The old London and Blackwall Railway brick viaduct on the west leg has been retained with significant internal renovation where it is two tracked. The section west of Limehouse where joint usage with National Rail services occurs was not rebuilt. This length of track was taken over in situ and also utilised the original rails and sleepers. Tunnels and curvature of radius lower than 100m are always mounted on slab to ensure security of position. Curvature greater than 100m where there is also significant gradient or has other need to ensure positional accuracy is also mounted on slab.

When DLR was originally constructed cost saving was achieved in using a rail weight and cross section smaller than general railway standards for what was correctly defined as a Light Railway. When rolled in quantity this gave significant cost savings. Thus BS80A rail was used and has been used for all the extensions to date. The tracks taken over directly from British Rail on the four tracked brick viaduct of the west leg were normal 113lb per yard and were not changed. They are still in situ although rails have been renewed as needed.

The original railway used Pandrol 'e' clip fastenings to the base plates. Later extensions have introduced some other fittings. The base plates used vary considerably around the railway. For slab track base these are resiliently bolted to the slab by drilling the slab and grouting in the bolts with chemical curing adhesive filler. Hard rubber pads under the rails provide electrical insulation and resilience. For viaducts with very specific noise or vibration reduction needs there are local installations of special base plates. The Canary Wharf area was fitted with Cologne egg base plates when the track was changed for the major station construction needed for the developments there. The points at King George V also use Cologne eggs. The original Canary Wharf station never having been finished or opening had no special provision. The City Airport extension is fitted with track on concrete sleepers for the sections on embankment at the western end with Pandrol 'e' clips. The main length of the line is on viaduct and uses Pandrol 'Fastclip' fixings with base plates and pads designed for low noise transmission.

Rail is continuously welded for all the main lines. Since the signalling system does not require any use of the rails for detection all rails are cross bonded for reduction in traction power supply resistance. Rails are tension stressed but to ensure against compression forces being generated by high temperatures in the track or in any viaduct movement there are frequent expansion joints in the rails. DLR has a significant variety of track formations with many sections being of short length and needing to be allowed flexibility of movement for environmental changes.

For the depots there are fewer restrictions in track position and in wear. For Poplar depot in the original installation, this allowed for the use of reclaimed part worn main line. The points needed were never the less provided as 80lb per yard. Thus Poplar depot as a considerable mixture of track sections with the attendant range of joint plates. Most of Poplar depot has Pandrol clip rail fixings but the are sections with elastic rail spikes. All the sleepers are timber. For Beckton concrete sleepers are mostly used with Pandrol clips and all 80lb per yard rail. For points on 40m radius the sleepers are fixed together using steel channels to prevent temperature derived movement interrupting detection of the point blade positions.

Approved and Potential Extensions

Woolwich Arsenal Extension

The extension to London City Airport and King George V is in that part of Docklands known historically as North Woolwich. The connections between Woolwich and North Woolwich are poor. There is an under-river pedestrian tunnel and a river ferry service which has vehicle carrying capacity, but no public transport through service. The alignment from King George V was built to go immediately onwards and downwards under the river in a semicircle to a below surface but open air terminus. This 2.5km extension was contracted for and work started in the summer of 2005. There will be only one station, which will be at Woolwich Arsenal alongside the existing National Rail station. This connection will create another cross-river axis and the most easterly urban rail service under the Thames. This is targeted for 2009 opening.

North London Line Conversion

Within Docklands and the connected deprived area along the valley of the River Lea is the present railway line between Stratford and North Woolwich that originated as part of the North London Railway. It was essentially moribund until the then Greater London Council was able to justify electrification in 1985, having had a minimal service following the closure of docks. The electrification in 1985, with services being a continuation of the established North London line electric services, was a great success in connecting up the areas served. The service demand north of Stratford has risen greatly but that south of Stratford has been much lower. This in part has been a result of single line working at the outer end restricting the service interval possible. The greater problem has been the failure to provide any new stations to attract custom from the residential areas and the remaining industrial employment. The outer end of the line will suffer more decline as traffic builds up on the DLR extension to North Woolwich.

DLR, with Transport for London, has made a case for transfer of the Stratford to North Woolwich section to DLR and conversion of most of it to DLR operation. Transport and Works Act process commenced on 31st August 2005 for expected approval by late 2006 and completion in 2009/2010. The exact layout and services operated have yet to be agreed, but the plans include a number of extra stations including the site of Stratford Market station now to be called Stratford High Street.

The main difference in service will be the extension to Stratford International over a new alignment with an intermediate station north of Stratford Regional as the present station will become named. The overall length will be 5km. The present track from Custom House to North Woolwich will not be converted as the area is already part of the recent DLR extension to City Airport.

Stratford Regional New Platforms

The approved line extension at Stratford is for a new position terminus with two platforms in place of the existing single narrow platform. Contracts were signed on 6th June 2005. Targets for the first platform are December 2006. On completion of this the service will be transferred whilst the second platform is completed for March 2007. Transfer with only one platform available is necessary to get the safety of the wider platform.

Dagenham Dock

DLR and TfL are working on an extension of the DLR to Barking Riverside and Dagenham Dock which is planned for completion around 2016. Three initial route options have been developed which will be subject to further development, consultation and review. The estimated cost for the project is approximately £235 million and at least four new stations will be built including a terminus station linking into the existing C2C station at Dagenham Dock to enable passengers to quickly interchange between services. TfL has held preliminary discussions with stakeholders including the London Boroughs of Newham and Barking & Dagenham, the Port of London Authority, the Office of the Deputy Prime Minister, Thames Gateway London Partnership, the Environment Agency and various transport authorities and landowners in the area..

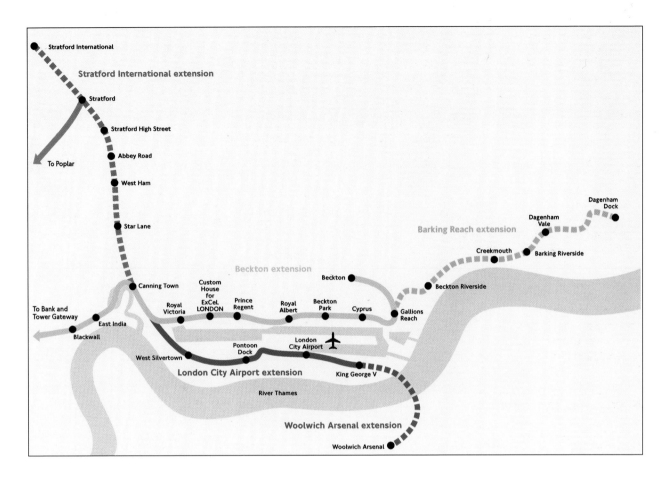

Stratford International

Stratford International extension

Stratford

Stratford High Street

To Poplar

Abbey Road

West Ham

Star Lane

Dagenham Dock

Dagenham Vale

Barking Reach extension

Creekmouth

Barking Riverside

Canning Town

Beckton Riverside

Beckton extension

Beckton

To Bank and Tower Gateway

East India

Blackwall

Royal Victoria

Custom House for ExCeL LONDON

Prince Regent

Royal Albert

Beckton Park

Cyprus

Gallions Reach

West Silvertown

Pontoon Dock

London City Airport

King George V

London City Airport extension

River Thames

Woolwich Arsenal extension

Woolwich Arsenal

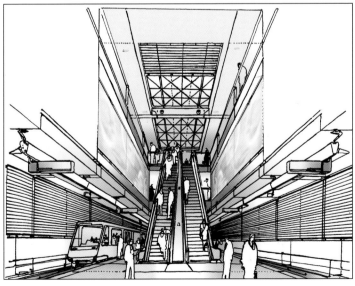

Above Future extensions to the DLR, the Woolwich Arsenal work already in progress.

Left A drawing of the sub–surface station designed for Woolwich Arsenal.

Looking towards Poplar station at Millwall Junction on the Great Eastern Railway in 1956.

Local railway history

About three-quarters of the initial DLR system opened in 1987 re-used old railway routes. Some of these older railways had been disused for many years; others remained in service up to the day the DLR took over the tracks. The origin, development and decay of these railways is closely tied up with the history of the up-river docks.

The City route

In 1836 an Act of Parliament was passed authorising the construction of 'The Commercial Railway' running from Minories, by the City Wall, 3½miles east to Brunswick Wharf at Blackwall. The railway passed close by the Regents Canal Dock, the West India Docks and the East India Docks. The railway was not initially intended to handle freight; rather it sought to attract large numbers of passengers whose journey from London to the Docks had

until then to be made either by river – slow and often circuitous – or by road, which was even slower. Before the introduction of the telegraph, all messages had to be conveyed by hand and a continuous stream of clerks, messenger boys and businessmen travelled to and from the Docks daily. Additionally, the increasing popularity of the seaside had resulted in a growing number of steamer services from London to Kent and Essex resorts; services which could operate far more cheaply and efficiently if they started from Blackwall rather than from the Pool of London.

Two rival schemes had been put before Parliament for very similar routes to the docks and the unsuccessful rivals eventually merged with the Commercial Railway, with George Stephenson and George Bidder becoming the Company's engineers. In 1839, a year after construction had started, the company received parliamentary approval for an extension from Minories to Fenchurch Street and a formal change of name to the London & Blackwall Railway.

Opening on 4th July 1840, the London & Blackwall Railway was in its day a sophisticated and rapid system. Carried mainly on a 4,020-yard viaduct – the cheapest way of building in a congested urban area – the double-tracked railway was cable-hauled using a drum-to-drum system and seven miles of hemp rope for each track, with winding engines at either end of the line.

Within two years of opening the railway had extended into the City to Fenchurch Street and was experimenting with goods traffic. It was however isolated from the rest of the growing London rail network by virtue of its wide track gauge and cable haulage, the cables having a tendency to occasionally twist or snap, despite now being metal instead of hemp. To expand further the railway needed to standardise its equipment. In 1845 parliament passed an Extension Act for the London & Blackwall Railway, authorising a connection with the Eastern Counties Railway at Bow and the change of gauge and haulage. The last cable-hauled train ran in 1849.

The Beckton route

Between Poplar and Beckton the DLR uses an all-new alignment.

Poplar to Stratford

The Eastern Counties Railway was incorporated in 1836, to run from Shoreditch to Norwich and Yarmouth. Within the London area the Eastern Counties Railway helped promote and then build the branch line from Stratford to North Woolwich in 1846/7 and had established at Stratford what was to become a major railway works. The London & Blackwall now became part of the growing Eastern Counties network, being eventually leased completely in 1865 to the Eastern Counties Railway, by now termed the Great Eastern Railway.

Other railways besides the Eastern Counties wanted to share in the lucrative docks traffic, and it was through a rival company, the North London Railway, that the DLR section from Bow Church to All Saints came to be built. The North London Railway (NLR) started in 1846 as the East & West India Docks and Birmingham Junction Railway Company. The intention was to build a freight line linking the docks with the London to Birmingham line at Chalk Farm in north London. It took four years to build and open the line as far south as Bow, and it was not until 1851 that the railway reached Poplar. Poplar Dock was served by a large goods depot and an extensive yard of sidings with over 14 miles of track. Part of this area is now occupied by the DLR Operations and Maintenance Centre.

Passing through some of the more prosperous new suburbs of London, the railway company carried passengers from the start, although it was not until 1866 that passenger services extended south of Bow. The heyday of the North London Railway occurred in the last twenty years of the 19th century. Over its Poplar line ran three other major railway companies' freight trains, and around Poplar Docks were grouped huge warehouses.

West India Quay to Lewisham

In complete contrast to the NLR was the tiny neighbouring Millwall Extension Railway, the route of which is now used by the DLR from Crossharbour to Island Gardens. It began back in 1865 when construction work started on the Millwall Dock. Millwall Dock was built with an internal rail network, designed around horse-hauled wagons – steam locomotives were too much of a fire risk with quaysides of wooden ships, often with canvas sails.

At around the same time, the Great Eastern Railway and the Millwall Canal Company (owners of the Millwall Dock) jointly proposed a railway which would develop the southern part of the Isle of Dogs. Running south from Millwall Junction at the top of the Isle of Dogs, the line would skirt the east side of West India Docks and pass alongside the Millwall Dock to terminate on the bank of the Thames close by the jetty for the ferry to Greenwich.

Although this railway, the Millwall Extension Railway, would benefit its promoters, the neighbouring East & West India Docks saw the line as a threat, abstracting traffic, and they objected vigorously. Thus it was that the Millwall Extension Railway, single track throughout, took six years to build, opening in 1871 to Millwall Docks and in 1872 to North Greenwich Station situated above the present-day Island Gardens Station. The DLR between Mudchute and Lewisham follows a route new to railway operation.

Canning Town to Woolwich

No old railway land is used for this route.

↘ **Arrivals**

12:00	LONDON CITY AIRPORT	ON TIME
12:06	CANNING TOWN	ON TIME
12:12	POPLAR	ON TIME
12:22	BANK	ON TIME

Now landed…

The extension to London City Airport has opened – ahead of schedule – with four new stations.

Connecting with buses, national rail and the Underground, the new route provides a fast and reliable service between the Airport, Canary Wharf and the City and is an important addition to DLR's growing network.

DLR maintains the highest standards of reliability, customer satisfaction and a commitment to integrated transport. With proposals for yet more expansion – the sky's the limit!

Time flies – with DLR

www.dlr.co.uk

MAYOR OF LONDON

Transport for London